COOKING CLASS
DESSERTS
COOKBOOK

PUBLICATIONS INTERNATIONAL, LTD.

Pyrex is a registered trademark of Corning Incorporated, Corning, NY 14831.

Photography on page 69 by Vuksanovich, Chicago.

Remaining photography by Sacco Productions Limited, Chicago.

Pictured on the front cover: Chocolate Chip Cake (*page 32*)
Pictured on the inside front cover: Raspberry Cheesecake Blossoms (*page 72*)
Pictured on the back cover: Mixed Berry Pie (*page 8*)

ISBN: 0-7853-0788-5

Manufactured in U.S.A.

8 7 6 5 4 3 2 1

Microwave Cooking: Microwave ovens vary in wattage. The microwave cooking times given in this publication are approximate. Use the cooking times as guidelines and check for doneness before adding more time. Consult manufacturer's instructions for suitable microwave-safe cooking dishes.

The publishers would like to thank the following companies and organizations for the use of their recipes in this publication: Black Walnut Bake-Off, Borden Kitchens, Borden, Inc., California Apricot Advisory Board, California State Fair, Celebrate Kansas Food Recipe Contest, Cherry Marketing Institute, Inc., Dole Food Company, Inc., Illinois State Fair, Thomas J. Lipton Co., Michigan Apple Committee, National Orange Show, Nebraska State Fair, New Mexico State Fair, North Dakota Wheat Commission, Pollio Dairy Products, The Procter and Gamble Company, The Quaker Oats Company, Southeast United Dairy Industry Association, Inc., Uncle Ben's Rice and Vermont Maple Festival.

CONTENTS

Chocolate Hazelnut Pie (page 23)

Simple Spumoni (page 44)

Ginger & Pear Tart (page 68)

CLASS NOTES

A fabulous dessert adds a special touch to any meal and this collection is sure to please. You'll marvel at the variety of desserts—cakes, pies, soufflés and mousses—and the multitude of flavors, such as vanilla, caramel, cherry, peanut butter, apple, strawberry, maple and, of course, chocolate!

Success in the kitchen is often achieved through careful organization and preparation. Before you begin a recipe, carefully read through the instructions, then gather all the ingredients and equipment. Do not make ingredient substitutions unless specifically called for in the recipe. Substitutions can alter the delicate balance of ingredients and the result may be less than perfect. Mastering the following skills will help ensure success in dessert-making every time.

BAKING TIPS

• Measure all ingredients carefully and accurately. To measure flour, spoon it lightly into a dry measuring cup and level it off with a straight-edge metal spatula (do not shake it down or tap it on the counter).

• Use the pan size specified in each recipe and prepare the pan as stated. The wrong size pan may cause the dessert to burn on the edges and bottom or sink in the middle.

• Oven temperatures may vary, so watch your dessert carefully and check for doneness using the test given in the recipe.

PASTRY MAKING TIPS

• Cut the shortening, margarine or butter into the flour and salt using a pastry blender or two knives until the mixture forms pea-sized pieces. Add the liquid, 1 tablespoon at a time, tossing lightly with a fork, until the dough is just moist enough to hold together when pressed.

• If the dough is sticky and difficult to handle, refrigerate it until firm. The easiest way to roll out pastry dough without sticking is to use a rolling pin cover and pastry cloth. Lightly flour the covered rolling pin and pastry cloth before using, and handle the dough quickly and lightly. A tough pie crust is often the result of too much flour worked into the dough or overhandling.

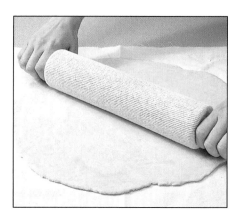

• Roll the dough out to a ⅛-inch-thick circle at least 1 inch larger than an inverted pie plate. To transfer dough to pie plate, place the rolling pin on one side of the dough. Gently roll the dough over the rolling pin once. Carefully lift the rolling pin and the dough, unrolling the dough over the pie plate. Ease the dough into the pie plate with fingertips and gently press into place. Be careful not to pull or stretch the dough, as this will cause it to shrink during baking.

- Often a pie crust is "baked blind," which means it is baked before the filling is added. To keep the pastry from puffing up during baking, line the crust with foil and fill it with dried beans, uncooked rice, or ceramic or metal pie weights. Bake the crust until set. Remove the foil and weights and either return the crust to the oven to finish baking or cool it completely before adding filling.

BEATING EGG WHITES

- Eggs separate more easily when cold, but egg whites reach their fullest volume if allowed to stand at room temperature for 30 minutes before beating.

- When beating egg whites, always check that the bowl and beaters are completely clean and dry. The smallest trace of yolk, water or fat can prevent the whites from obtaining maximum volume. For best results, use a copper, stainless steel or glass bowl (plastic bowls may have an oily film, even after repeated washings).

- Beat the whites slowly until they are foamy, then increase the speed. Add a pinch of salt and cream of tartar at this point to help stabilize them. Do not overbeat or they will become dry and clump together.

- Beat the egg whites to the desired stage. For soft peaks, lift the beaters from the egg whites; they should form droopy, but definite, peaks. For stiff peaks, lift the beaters from the egg whites; stiff peaks should remain on the surface and the mixture will not slide around when the bowl is tilted.

- Immediately fold beaten egg whites gently into another mixture so volume is not lost; never beat or stir. To fold egg whites into another mixture, add egg whites and with a rubber spatula gently cut down to the bottom of the bowl. Then, scrape up side of bowl and fold over the top of the mixture. Repeat until the egg whites are fully incorporated.

DISSOLVING GELATIN

- To dissolve unflavored gelatin successfully, sprinkle one envelope of gelatin over ¼ cup of cold liquid in a small saucepan. Let it stand for 3 minutes to soften. Stir over low heat about 5 minutes or until the gelatin is completely dissolved.

- Run a finger over the spoon to test for undissolved gelatin granules. If it is smooth, the gelatin is completely dissolved; if it feels granular, continue heating until it feels smooth.

WHIPPING CREAM

- For best results when beating whipping or heavy cream, first chill the cream, bowl and beaters—the cold keeps the fat in the cream solid, thus increasing the volume.

- For optimum volume, beat the cream in a deep, narrow bowl. Generally 1 cup of cream will yield 2 cups of whipped cream, so be sure to choose a bowl that will accommodate the increased volume. Beat the cream until soft peaks form. To test, lift the beaters from the whipping cream; the mixture should form droopy, but definite, peaks. Do not overbeat or the cream will clump together and form butter.

Mixed Berry Pie

Classic Double Pie Crust (page 29)
2 cups canned or thawed frozen blackberries, well drained
1½ cups canned or thawed frozen blueberries, well drained
½ cup canned or thawed frozen gooseberries, well drained
¼ cup sugar
3 tablespoons cornstarch
⅛ teaspoon almond extract

1. Prepare pie crust following steps 1 and 2 of Classic Double Pie Crust (page 29). Roll out and place bottom crust in pie plate following steps 3 through 6. Cover with plastic wrap and refrigerate 30 minutes to allow dough to relax.

2. Preheat oven to 425°F.

3. Combine blackberries, blueberries and gooseberries in large bowl. Add sugar, cornstarch and almond extract; stir well.

4. Spoon into prepared pie crust. Roll out top crust following step 4 on page 29. Place top crust over filling following step 7.

5. Trim edge leaving ½-inch overhang. Fold overhang under so crust is even with edge of pie plate. Press between thumb and forefinger to make stand-up edge. Cut slits in crust at ½-inch intervals around edge of pie to form flaps.

6. Press 1 flap in toward center of pie and the next out toward rim of pie plate. Continue alternating in and out around edge of pie.

7. Pierce top crust with fork to allow steam to escape.

8. Bake 40 minutes or until crust is golden brown. Cool completely on wire rack.

Makes 6 to 8 servings

Step 4. Unrolling top crust over filling.

Step 5. Cutting slits in crust.

Step 6. Pressing flap in toward center of pie.

Topsy Turvy Apple Pie

¼ cup butter or margarine, softened
½ cup pecan halves
½ cup packed brown sugar
  Classic Double Pie Crust (page 29)
4 large Granny Smith apples
1 tablespoon lemon juice
1 tablespoon all-purpose flour
½ cup granulated sugar
1 teaspoon ground cinnamon
1 teaspoon ground nutmeg
  Dash salt

1. Spread butter evenly on bottom and up side of 9-inch pie plate. Press pecans, rounded side down, into butter. Pat brown sugar on pecans.

2. Prepare pie crust following steps 1 and 2 of Classic Double Pie Crust (page 29). Roll out and place bottom crust in pie plate following steps 3 through 6. Cover with plastic wrap and refrigerate 30 minutes to allow dough to relax.

3. Preheat oven to 400°F.

4. Peel apples. Remove cores; discard. Cut apples into slices.

5. Place apple slices in large bowl; sprinkle with lemon juice. Combine flour, granulated sugar, cinnamon, nutmeg and salt in small bowl. Add to apples; toss to coat.

6. Place apple mixture in pie crust; spread evenly to make top level.

7. Roll out top crust following step 4 on page 29. Place top crust over filling following step 7.

8. Trim edge leaving ½-inch overhang. Fold overhang under so crust is even with edge of pie plate. Press flat to seal. Flute, if desired. Pierce top crust with fork to allow steam to escape.

9. Bake 50 minutes. Remove from oven; cool 5 minutes on wire rack.

10. Place serving dish over warm pie plate. Invert both pie plate and serving dish so serving dish is on the bottom. Remove pie plate. Serve pie warm or at room temperature.

Makes 6 to 8 servings

Step 1. Patting brown sugar on pecans.

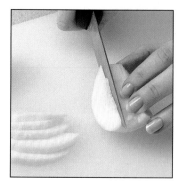

Step 4. Cutting apples into slices.

Step 10. Removing pie plate after inverting pie.

My Golden Harvest Apple Pie

**Classic Double Pie Crust
   (page 29)**
2 tablespoons all-purpose flour
2 pounds apples
½ cup sugar
1 teaspoon ground cinnamon
1 teaspoon ground nutmeg
**3 tablespoons low-sugar orange
   marmalade**
**2 tablespoons butter or
   margarine**
Milk

1. Prepare pie crust following steps 1 and 2 of Classic Double Pie Crust (page 29). Roll out and place bottom crust in pie plate following steps 3 through 6. Cover with plastic wrap and refrigerate 30 minutes to allow dough to relax. Sprinkle crust with flour.

2. Preheat oven to 450°F.

3. Peel apples. Remove cores; discard. Thinly slice apples. (Technique on page 10).

4. Combine sugar, cinnamon and nutmeg in small bowl. Layer apple slices alternately with sugar mixture in pie crust.

5. Drop marmalade by teaspoonfuls on top of apples. Cut butter into 10 pieces. Place butter pieces on top of apples in pie crust.

6. Roll out top crust following step 4 on page 29. Place top crust over filling following step 7.

7. Trim edge leaving ½-inch overhang. Fold overhang under so crust is even with edge of pie plate.

8. To flute, place index finger on inside edge of rim, pointing toward outside of pie. Pinch crust into "V" shape between index finger and thumb of other hand. Repeat along edge.

9. Cut out designs in top crust with paring knife. Reroll dough scraps and cut out stem and leaf shapes. Brush top crust with milk. Place shapes on pie.

10. Bake 15 minutes. *Reduce oven temperature to 375°F.* Continue baking 30 to 35 minutes or until golden brown. Cool completely on wire rack. *Makes 6 to 8 servings*

Step 5. Dropping marmalade on top of apples.

Step 8. Fluting edge of pie crust.

Step 9. Cutting out stem and leaf shapes.

Mississippi Mist Pie

1 package (8 ounces) light cream cheese
6 to 8 limes
50 vanilla wafer cookies
5 tablespoons butter or margarine, melted
2 pints fresh strawberries
1 can (14 ounces) sweetened condensed milk
1 tablespoon green creme de menthe liqueur
Sweetened Whipped Cream (page 16)
Lime slices for garnish

1. Place light cream cheese on opened package on cutting board. With utility knife, cut cream cheese lengthwise into ½-inch slices. Then cut crosswise into ½-inch pieces. Let stand at room temperature until softened. (Cream cheese will be easy to push down.)

2. To juice limes, cut limes in half on cutting board.

3. Using citrus reamer, squeeze juice from limes into measuring cup or small bowl. Measure ½ cup lime juice. Set aside.

4. Place cookies in food processor or blender container; process using on/off pulses until finely crushed.

5. Combine cookie crumbs and butter in medium bowl; mix well. Press firmly onto bottom and up side of 9-inch pie plate. Refrigerate until firm.

continued on page 16

Step 1. Softening cream cheese.

Step 3. Juicing limes.

Step 4. Processing cookies in food processor.

6. Reserve 3 strawberries for garnish. Cut green tops off remaining strawberries so that they are no more than 1 inch tall. Arrange strawberries, cut ends down, on crust; refrigerate.

7. Beat cream cheese in large bowl with electric mixer at medium speed until smooth, scraping down side of bowl once. Add sweetened condensed milk; beat at medium speed until smooth. Add lime juice and liqueur; beat at low speed until well blended.

8. Pour into prepared crust, covering strawberries. Refrigerate at least 1 hour.

9. Prepare Sweetened Whipped Cream. Spoon into pastry bag fitted with star decorating tip. Pipe lattice design on top of pie.

10. Slice reserved strawberries. Garnish, if desired.   *Makes 6 to 8 servings*

Sweetened Whipped Cream

1 cup whipping cream
3 tablespoons sugar
½ teaspoon vanilla

1. Chill large bowl and beaters thoroughly. Pour chilled whipping cream into chilled bowl and beat with electric mixer at high speed until soft peaks form. To test, lift beaters from whipping cream; mixture should have droopy, but definite, peaks.

2. Gradually add sugar and vanilla. Whip until stiff peaks form. To test, lift beaters from cream mixture; stiff peaks should remain on surface.

Step 6. Arranging strawberries on crust.

Step 9. Piping lattice design on top of pie.

Sweetened Whipped Cream: Step 2. Testing for stiff peaks.

Heavenly Sinful Lemon Chiffon Pie

2 or 3 lemons
  Lemon Crust (page 18)
4 eggs*
1 cup sugar, divided
½ teaspoon unflavored gelatin
¼ teaspoon salt
  Sweetened Whipped Cream
    (page 16)
  Lemon peel and mint leaf for
    garnish

*Use clean, uncracked eggs.

1. Finely grate colored portion of lemon peel using bell grater or hand-held grater. Measure 2 tablespoons; set aside. Reserve 1 tablespoon remaining lemon peel for Lemon Crust.

2. To juice lemons, cut lemons in half on cutting board.

3. Using citrus reamer, squeeze juice from lemons into measuring cup or small bowl. Measure ⅓ cup juice. Reserve 1 teaspoon remaining juice for Lemon Crust.

4. Prepare Lemon Crust; set aside.

5. To separate egg yolk from white, gently tap egg in center against hard surface, such as side of bowl. Holding shell half in each hand, gently transfer yolk back and forth between the 2 shell halves. Allow white to drip down between the 2 halves into bowl.

6. When all white has dripped into bowl, place yolk in another bowl. Transfer white to third bowl. Repeat with remaining 3 eggs. (Egg whites must be free from any egg yolk to reach the proper volume when beaten.)

7. Beat 4 egg yolks in small bowl with wire whisk until thick and lemon colored.

8. Combine ½ cup sugar and gelatin in top of double boiler. Add beaten egg yolks, 2 tablespoons lemon peel and lemon juice to gelatin mixture; mix well. Let stand without stirring 3 minutes for gelatin to soften.

continued on page 18

Step 1. Grating lemon peel.

Step 5. Separating egg yolk from white.

***Heavenly Sinful Lemon Chiffon Pie,
continued***

9. Heat mixture over hot, not boiling, water, stirring constantly, until gelatin is completely dissolved, about 10 minutes. To test for undissolved gelatin, run a finger over the spoon. If it is smooth, the gelatin is completely dissolved; if it feels granular, continue heating until it feels smooth. Remove from heat.

10. To make meringue, combine egg whites and salt in clean large bowl. Beat with electric mixer at high speed until foamy. Gradually beat in remaining ½ cup sugar until stiff peaks form. After beaters are lifted from meringue, stiff peaks should remain on surface, and mixture will not slide around when bowl is tilted.

11. Fold egg white mixture into gelatin mixture with rubber spatula by gently cutting down to bottom of bowl, scraping up side of bowl, then folding over top of mixture. Repeat until egg whites are evenly incorporated. Pour into cooled crust.

12. Prepare Sweetened Whipped Cream. Spoon into pastry bag fitted with star decorating tip. Pipe along edge of pie. Garnish, if desired.

Makes 1 (9-inch) pie

Lemon Crust

1 cup all-purpose flour
¼ cup sugar
**1 tablespoon reserved grated lemon
  peel**
½ cup butter
1 egg yolk (technique on page 17)
½ teaspoon vanilla
1 teaspoon reserved lemon juice

1. Preheat oven to 400°F.

2. Combine flour, sugar and grated lemon peel in medium bowl.

3. Cut in butter with pastry blender or 2 knives until mixture forms pea-sized pieces.

4. Combine egg yolk, vanilla and lemon juice in small bowl; beat until well combined. Add to flour mixture; mix well.

5. Press evenly into 9-inch pie plate. Pierce pie crust with fork at ¼-inch intervals, about 40 times. (Technique on page 78.)

6. Cut a square of foil about 4 inches larger than pie plate. Line pie crust with foil. Fill with dried beans, uncooked rice or ceramic pie weights. (Technique on page 20.)

7. Bake 10 minutes or until set. Remove from oven. Gently remove foil lining and beans. Cool completely on wire rack.

Step 10. Testing for stiff peaks.

Step 12. Piping Sweetened Whipped Cream around edge of pie.

Lemon Crust: Step 3. Cutting butter into flour mixture.

Norma Gene's Peanut Butter Creme Pie

Classic Single Pie Crust
  (page 28)
3 eggs
¾ cup granulated sugar, divided
3 tablespoons cornstarch
1 tablespoon all-purpose flour
⅛ teaspoon salt
3 cups milk
2 teaspoons butter or margarine
1 teaspoon vanilla
¾ cup powdered sugar
½ cup crunchy peanut butter
¼ teaspoon cream of tartar

1. Prepare pie crust following steps 1 and 2 of Classic Single Pie Crust (page 28). Roll out and place in pie plate following steps 3 through 7.

2. Trim dough leaving ¼-inch overhang. Fold overhang under and press flat. Cut ½-inch slits at 1-inch intervals around edge of pie crust with scissors.

3. Fold dough flap under on a diagonal at each slit to form a point. Cover pie crust with plastic wrap and refrigerate 30 minutes to allow dough to relax.

4. Preheat oven to 425°F.

5. Pierce pie crust with fork at ¼-inch intervals, about 40 times. (Technique on page 78.)

6. Cut a square of foil about 4 inches larger than pie plate. Line pie crust with foil. Fill with dried beans, uncooked rice or ceramic pie weights.

7. Bake 10 minutes or until set. Remove from oven. Gently remove foil lining and beans. Return pie crust to oven and bake 5 minutes or until very light brown. Cool completely on wire rack. *Reduce oven temperature to 375°F.*

8. To separate egg yolk from white, gently tap egg in center against hard surface, such as side of bowl. Holding shell half in each hand, gently transfer yolk back and forth between the 2 shell halves. Allow white to drip down between the 2 halves into bowl. (Technique on page 17.)

continued on page 22

Step 2. Cutting slits in crust.

Step 3. Folding dough flaps under.

Step 6. Filling lined pie crust with dried beans.

Norma Gene's Peanut Butter Creme Pie, continued

9. When all white has dripped into bowl, place yolk in another bowl. Transfer white to third bowl. Repeat with remaining 2 eggs. (Egg whites must be free from any egg yolk to reach proper volume when beaten.)

10. To make filling, stir together ½ cup granulated sugar, cornstarch, flour and salt in medium saucepan. Add egg yolks and milk; beat with wire whisk until well blended. Bring to a boil over medium heat, stirring constantly. Continue cooking and stirring 2 minutes or until thick. Remove from heat. Stir in butter and vanilla.

11. Place powdered sugar in medium bowl. Cut peanut butter into powdered sugar with pastry blender or 2 knives until mixture forms pea-sized pieces.

12. Sprinkle ⅓ of peanut butter crumbs over pie crust. Spoon ½ of filling over crumbs. Sprinkle with another ⅓ of crumbs; top with remaining filling.

13. To make meringue, combine egg whites and cream of tartar in clean large bowl. Beat with electric mixer at high speed until foamy. Gradually beat in remaining ¼ cup granulated sugar until stiff peaks form. After beaters are lifted from meringue, stiff peaks should remain on surface, and mixture will not slide around when bowl is tilted. (Technique on page 18.)

14. Spread meringue over pie filling with rubber spatula, making sure it completely covers filling and touches edge of pie crust.

15. Create decorative peaks and swirls by twisting and lifting spatula while spreading meringue. Sprinkle remaining peanut butter crumbs around edge.

16. Bake 8 to 10 minutes or until meringue is golden. Cool completely on wire rack.   *Makes 6 to 8 servings*

Step 11. Cutting peanut butter into powdered sugar.

Step 14. Spreading meringue over pie filling.

Step 15. Creating decorative peaks and swirls.

Chocolate Hazelnut Pie

**Chocolate Hazelnut Crust
(page 24)
1 envelope unflavored gelatin
¼ cup cold water
2 cups whipping cream, divided
1½ cups semisweet chocolate chips
2 eggs*
3 tablespoons hazelnut-flavored
liqueur
1 teaspoon vanilla
24 caramels, unwrapped
Caramel Flowers for garnish
(page 24)**

*Use clean, uncracked eggs.

1. Prepare Chocolate Hazelnut Crust; set aside.

2. Sprinkle gelatin over water in small saucepan. Let stand without stirring 3 minutes for gelatin to soften. Heat over low heat, stirring constantly, until gelatin is completely dissolved, about 5 minutes. To test for undissolved gelatin, run a finger over the spoon. If it is smooth, the gelatin is completely dissolved; if it feels granular, continue heating until it feels smooth.

3. Stir 1 cup whipping cream into gelatin mixture. Heat just to a boil; remove from heat. Add chocolate chips. Stir until chocolate is melted.

4. Add ½ cup whipping cream, eggs, liqueur and vanilla; beat well. Pour into large bowl; refrigerate about 15 minutes or until thickened.

5. Combine caramels and remaining ½ cup whipping cream in small saucepan. Simmer over low heat, stirring occasionally, until completely melted and smooth.

6. Pour caramel mixture into prepared crust; let stand about 10 minutes.

7. Beat thickened gelatin mixture with electric mixer at medium speed until smooth. Pour over caramel layer; refrigerate 3 hours or until firm. Garnish, if desired.

Makes 6 to 8 servings

continued on page 24

Step 2. Testing for undissolved gelatin.

Step 3. Stirring until chocolate is melted.

Step 5. Stirring until caramel is melted and smooth.

Chocolate Hazelnut Crust

¾ cup hazelnuts
30 chocolate cookie wafers
½ cup melted butter or margarine

1. Preheat oven to 350°F.

2. To toast hazelnuts, spread hazelnuts in single layer on baking sheet. Bake 10 to 12 minutes or until toasted and skins begin to flake off; let cool slightly. Wrap hazelnuts in heavy kitchen towel; rub towel back and forth to remove as much of the skins as possible.

3. Combine cookies and hazelnuts in food processor or blender container; process with on/off pulses until finely crushed.

4. Combine cookie crumb mixture and butter in medium bowl. Press firmly onto bottom and up side of 9-inch pie plate, forming a high rim.

5. Bake 10 minutes; cool completely on wire rack.

Caramel Flowers

6 to 8 caramels

1. Place 1 fresh, soft caramel between 2 sheets of waxed paper.

2. With rolling pin, roll out caramel to 2-inch oval (press down hard with rolling pin).

3. Starting at 1 corner, roll caramel into a cone to resemble a flower. Repeat with remaining caramels. Before serving, place 1 Caramel Flower on each piece of pie.

Chocolate Hazelnut Crust: Step 2. Rubbing skins off toasted hazelnuts.

Caramel Flowers: Step 2. Rolling caramel out to 2-inch oval.

Caramel Flowers: Step 3. Rolling caramel into a cone.

White Russian Pie

40 chocolate cookie wafers,
　crushed (page 14)
5 tablespoons butter or
　margarine, melted
7 tablespoons coffee-flavored
　liqueur, divided
1 envelope Knox® Unflavored
　Gelatine
6 tablespoons sugar, divided
3 eggs, separated (technique on
　page 17)
½ cup water
¼ cup vodka
1 cup whipping cream, whipped
　(technique on page 56)
　Chocolate Curls for garnish
　(page 58)

1. Preheat oven to 350°F.

2. Combine cookie crumbs, butter and 4 tablespoons coffee liqueur in medium bowl. Press firmly onto bottom and up side of 9-inch pie plate. Bake 3 minutes; cool completely on wire rack.

3. Combine gelatine and 4 tablespoons sugar in small saucepan. Combine egg yolks and water in small bowl; beat well. Add to gelatine mixture. Let stand without stirring 3 minutes for gelatine to soften.

4. Heat over low heat, stirring constantly, until gelatine is completely dissolved, about 5 minutes. (Technique on page 23.)

5. Stir in vodka and remaining 3 tablespoons coffee liqueur. Pour mixture into large bowl. Place bowl in refrigerator; stir mixture occasionally. Chill until mixture mounds slightly when dropped from spoon. Remove from refrigerator.

6. Beat egg whites with remaining 2 tablespoons sugar until stiff peaks form. (Technique on page 18.)

7. Fold egg white mixture into gelatine mixture with rubber spatula by gently cutting down to bottom of bowl, scraping up side of bowl, then folding over top of mixture. Repeat until egg whites are evenly incorporated.

8. Fold whipped cream into gelatine mixture as described in step 7. Spread into prepared crust; refrigerate until firm. Garnish, if desired.　　　*Makes 6 to 8 servings*

Step 2. Pressing crumb mixture onto bottom and up side of pie plate.

Step 4. Testing for undissolved gelatine.

Step 6. Testing for stiff peaks.

Classic Single Pie Crust

1⅓ **cups all-purpose flour**
½ **teaspoon salt**
½ **cup Crisco® Shortening**
3 **tablespoons cold water**

1. Combine flour and salt in large bowl. Cut in shortening using pastry blender or 2 knives until mixture forms pea-sized pieces.

2. Sprinkle with water, 1 tablespoon at a time. Toss with fork until mixture holds together. Press together to form a ball.

3. Press dough between hands to form 5- to 6-inch disk.

4. Lightly flour work surface and rolling pin. Roll dough in short strokes, starting in middle of disk and rolling out toward edge. Rotate dough ¼ turn to right. Sprinkle more flour under dough and on rolling pin as necessary to prevent sticking. Continue to roll and rotate dough 2 to 3 more times.

5. Roll dough into ⅛-inch-thick circle at least 1 inch larger than inverted pie plate.

6. Place rolling pin on 1 side of dough. Gently roll dough over rolling pin once.

7. Carefully lift rolling pin and dough. Unroll dough over pie plate. Ease dough into pie plate with fingertips. Do not stretch dough.

8. Trim crust, leaving ½-inch overhang. Fold overhang under. Flute as desired. Cover pie crust with plastic wrap and refrigerate 30 minutes to allow dough to relax.

Step 1. Cutting in shortening.

Step 3. Pressing dough into disk.

Step 4. Rolling out dough.

Classic Double Pie Crust

2 cups all-purpose flour
1 teaspoon salt
¾ cup Crisco® Shortening
5 tablespoons cold water

1. Combine flour and salt in large bowl. Cut in shortening using pastry blender or 2 knives until mixture forms pea-sized pieces.

2. Sprinkle with water, 1 tablespoon at a time. Toss with fork until mixture holds together. Press together to form a ball.

3. Divide dough in half. Press each half between hands to form 5- to 6-inch disk.

4. Roll out each half as described in Classic Single Pie Crust, steps 4 and 5.

5. Place rolling pin on 1 side of dough. Gently roll dough over rolling pin once. Carefully lift rolling pin and dough.

6. Unroll dough over pie plate. Ease dough into pie plate with fingertips. Do not stretch dough. Trim edge even with edge of pie crust. Cover pie crust with plastic wrap and refrigerate 30 minutes to allow dough to relax.

7. Add desired filling to unbaked pie crust. Moisten edge of crust with water. Lift top crust onto filled pie as described in step 5. Unroll over filling. Pierce top crust with fork to allow steam to escape.

8. Trim crust leaving ½-inch overhang. Fold overhang under bottom crust. Flute as desired.

Step 5. Lifting rolled out dough.

Step 6. Unrolling dough over pie plate.

Step 7. Unrolling top crust over filling.

Apple Butter Pound Cake

1½ cups granulated sugar
1 package (8 ounces) cream cheese, softened (technique on page 14)
½ cup margarine, softened
6 eggs
2 cups all-purpose flour
1 cup Quaker® Enriched Corn Meal
2 teaspoons baking powder
1 teaspoon ground cinnamon
¼ teaspoon salt (optional)
1 cup spiced apple butter
1 tablespoon bourbon whiskey (optional)
1 teaspoon vanilla
1 cup chopped pecans
Creamy Glaze (recipe follows)

1. Preheat oven to 350°F. Grease 12-cup Bundt pan.

2. Beat sugar, cream cheese and margarine in large bowl with electric mixer at medium speed until light and fluffy, scraping down side of bowl once.

3. Add eggs, 1 at a time, beating well after each addition.

4. Combine flour, corn meal, baking powder, cinnamon and salt in small bowl.

5. Combine apple butter, bourbon and vanilla in separate small bowl.

6. Alternately add flour mixture and apple butter mixture to cream cheese mixture. Beat at low speed until well blended, scraping down side of bowl once. Stir in pecans. Spoon into prepared pan; spread evenly to edge.

7. Bake 60 to 70 minutes or until wooden skewer or cake tester inserted in center comes out clean. Cool 10 minutes in pan. Remove from pan; cool completely on wire rack.

8. Prepare Creamy Glaze. Drizzle over cake from tip of spoon.   *Makes 10 to 12 servings*

Step 1. Greasing the pan.

Step 8. Drizzling Creamy Glaze over cake.

Creamy Glaze

1 cup powdered sugar
1½ teaspoons light corn syrup
¼ teaspoon vanilla or Bourbon whiskey
4 to 5 teaspoons milk

Combine powdered sugar, corn syrup and vanilla in medium bowl; mix well. Add milk, 1 teaspoon at a time, until proper drizzling consistency is reached.

Chocolate Chip Cake

2 cups all-purpose flour
1 cup packed dark brown sugar
1 tablespoon baking powder
1 teaspoon salt
½ teaspoon baking soda
½ cup granulated sugar
½ cup shortening
3 eggs
1¼ cups milk
1½ teaspoons vanilla
½ cup semisweet chocolate chips,
   finely chopped
   Butterscotch Filling (page 34)
   Chocolate Chip Glaze
   (page 34)
½ cup finely chopped walnuts,
   divided
   Fresh raspberries and mint
   leaves for garnish

1. Preheat oven to 350°F.

2. Grease bottom and sides of two 9-inch round baking pans. Add 2 to 3 teaspoons flour to each pan. Gently tap side of pan to evenly coat bottom and sides with flour.

3. Combine flour, brown sugar, baking powder, salt and baking soda in small bowl. Set aside.

4. Beat granulated sugar and shortening in large bowl with electric mixer at medium speed until light and fluffy, scraping down side of bowl once.

5. Add eggs, 1 at a time, beating well after each addition.

6. Add milk and vanilla; beat at low speed until well blended. Add flour mixture and chocolate chips. Beat at low speed until blended. Beat at medium speed until smooth, scraping bowl occasionally. Pour into prepared pans.

7. Bake 40 to 45 minutes or until cake tester or wooden pick inserted into center comes out clean. Remove from pan to wire rack; cool completely.

continued on page 34

Step 2. Coating pan with flour.

Step 4. Beating sugar and shortening together.

Step 6. Pouring batter into prepared pans.

Chocolate Chip Cake, continued

8. Prepare Butterscotch Filling and Chocolate Chip Glaze.

9. Place 1 cake layer on serving plate. Spread with Butterscotch Filling; sprinkle with ¼ cup walnuts. Top with second cake layer.

10. Pour Chocolate Chip Glaze over top of cake, allowing some of glaze to drip down side of cake. Sprinkle remaining ¼ cup walnuts on top. Garnish, if desired.

Makes 8 to 10 servings

Butterscotch Filling

½ cup packed light brown sugar
2 tablespoons cornstarch
¼ teaspoon salt
½ cup water
1 tablespoon butter

1. Combine brown sugar, cornstarch and salt in medium saucepan. Add water; cook over medium heat until mixture comes to a boil, stirring constantly. Boil 1 minute until mixture thickens, stirring constantly.

2. Add butter; stir until melted. Cool completely.

Chocolate Chip Glaze

½ cup semisweet chocolate chips
2 tablespoons butter
1 tablespoon light corn syrup

Combine chocolate chips, butter and corn syrup in small saucepan. Cook over low heat until chocolate melts, stirring constantly. Cool slightly.

Step 9. Sprinkling walnuts over Butterscotch Filling.

Step 10. Pouring Chocolate Chip Glaze over top of cake.

Butterscotch Filling: Step 1. Bringing brown sugar mixture to a boil.

Sour Cream Pound Cake

1 orange
1 cup butter, softened
2¾ cups sugar
1 tablespoon vanilla
6 eggs
3 cups all-purpose flour
½ teaspoon salt
¼ teaspoon baking soda
1 cup sour cream
Citrus Topping (page 36)

1. Preheat oven to 325°F. Grease 10-inch tube pan.

2. Finely grate colored portion of orange peel using bell grater or hand-held grater. Measure 2 teaspoons orange peel; set aside.

3. Beat butter in large bowl at medium speed of electric mixer until creamy, scraping down side of bowl once. Gradually add sugar, beating until light and fluffy. Beat in vanilla and orange peel.

4. Add eggs, 1 at a time, beating 1 minute after each addition.

5. Combine flour, salt and baking soda in small bowl. Add to butter mixture alternately with sour cream, beginning and ending with flour mixture. Beat well after each addition. Pour into prepared pan.

6. Bake 1 hour and 15 minutes or until cake tester or wooden skewer inserted in center comes out clean.

7. Prepare Citrus Topping. Spoon over hot cake; cool in pan 15 minutes. Remove from pan to wire rack, topping side up; cool completely. *Makes 10 to 12 servings*

continued on page 36

Step 2. Grating orange peel.

Step 3. Beating in orange peel.

Step 6. Testing cake for doneness.

Sour Cream Pound Cake, continued

Citrus Topping

2 oranges
2 teaspoons salt
½ cup sugar, divided
⅓ cup lemon juice
1 teaspoon vanilla

1. With citrus zester or vegetable peeler, remove colored peel, not white pith, from oranges. Measure ⅓ cup.

2. To juice oranges, cut oranges in half on cutting board.

3. Using citrus reamer, squeeze juice from oranges into measuring cup or small bowl. Measure ⅓ cup.

4. Combine orange peel and salt in medium saucepan. Add enough water to cover.

5. Bring to a boil over high heat. Boil 2 minutes. Drain in fine-meshed sieve. Return orange peel to saucepan.

6. Add orange juice and ¼ cup sugar to saucepan. Bring to a boil over high heat. Reduce heat; simmer 10 minutes. Remove from heat.

7. Add remaining ¼ cup sugar, lemon juice and vanilla; stir until smooth.

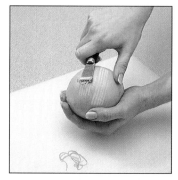

Citrus Topping: Step 1. Removing orange peel with citrus zester.

Citrus Topping: Step 4. Adding water to cover orange peel.

Citrus Topping: Step 5. Draining orange peel.

Carrot Cake

1¼ pounds carrots
4 eggs
1½ cups vegetable oil
2 cups all-purpose flour
2 cups sugar
2 teaspoons baking soda
2 teaspoons baking powder
2 teaspoons ground cinnamon
¼ teaspoon salt
1½ cups coarsely chopped pecans
   or walnuts
   Cream Cheese Icing
   (recipe follows)

1. Trim ends of carrots; discard. Peel carrots. Shred with shredding disk of food processor or hand shredder. Measure 3 cups; set aside.

2. Preheat oven to 350°F. Grease and flour sides of 13×9-inch baking pan. (Technique on page 32.)

3. Beat eggs and oil in small bowl. Combine flour, sugar, baking soda, baking powder, cinnamon and salt in large bowl. Add egg mixture; mix well. Stir in carrots and pecans. Pour into prepared pan.

4. Bake 30 to 35 minutes or until cake tester or wooden pick inserted in center comes out clean. Cool completely on wire rack.

5. Prepare Cream Cheese Icing. Spread over cooled cake. Garnish, if desired.

Makes 8 to 10 servings

Cream Cheese Icing

4 cups (16-ounce box) powdered sugar
1 package (8 ounces) cream cheese, softened
   (technique on page 14)
½ cup margarine, softened
1 teaspoon vanilla

1. Sift powdered sugar into large bowl with fine-meshed sieve or sifter.

2. Beat cream cheese, margarine and vanilla in another large bowl with electric mixer at medium speed until smooth, scraping down side of bowl occasionally.

3. Gradually add powdered sugar. Beat with electric mixer at low speed until well blended, scraping down side of bowl occasionally.

Makes about 1½ cups

Step 1. Shredding carrots in food processor.

Step 5. Spreading Cream Cheese Icing over cake.

Cream Cheese Icing: Step 1. Sifting powdered sugar.

Apricot Meringue Squares

1 orange
1 cup butter, softened
⅓ cup granulated sugar
1 teaspoon vanilla
2 cups all-purpose flour
1 jar (12 ounces) apricot jam
2 egg whites (technique on
    page 17)
1 cup powdered sugar
    Slivered almonds for garnish

1. Finely grate colored portion of orange peel using bell grater or hand-held grater. Measure 2 teaspoons orange peel; set aside.

2. To juice orange, cut orange in half on cutting board. Using citrus reamer, squeeze juice from orange into measuring cup or small bowl. Measure 2 tablespoons juice; set aside.

3. Preheat oven to 350°F.

4. Beat butter, granulated sugar, vanilla and orange peel in large bowl with electric mixer at medium speed until light and fluffy, scraping down side of bowl once. Gradually add flour, beating at low speed until smooth.

5. Press into ungreased 13 × 9-inch baking pan. Bake 15 minutes. Cool completely on wire rack.

6. Combine jam and orange juice in small bowl; beat until smooth. Spread over cooled crust.

7. To make meringue, beat egg whites in clean large bowl with electric mixer at high speed until foamy. Gradually beat in powdered sugar until stiff peaks form. After beaters are lifted from meringue, stiff peaks should remain on surface, and mixture will not slide around when bowl is tilted. (Technique on page 18.)

8. Spread meringue over jam mixture with rubber spatula.

9. Bake at 350°F 15 to 20 minutes or until light golden brown. Cool completely on wire rack. Cut into 2-inch squares. Garnish, if desired.   *Makes about 2 dozen squares*

Step 1. Grating orange peel.

Step 8. Spreading meringue over jam mixture.

Black Walnut Fudge

4 cups sugar
½ cup margarine
1 can (12 ounces) evaporated milk
3 tablespoons light corn syrup
1 pound vanilla milk chips*
1 jar (13 ounces) marshmallow creme
1 cup chopped black walnuts
1 tablespoon vanilla

*Do not use compound chocolate or confectioner's coating.

1. Line 13×9-inch pan with foil, leaving 1-inch overhang on sides to use for handles when lifting fudge out of pan. Lightly butter foil.

2. Combine sugar, margarine, evaporated milk and corn syrup in large saucepan; stir well. Bring to a boil over medium heat, stirring only until sugar dissolves.

3. Attach candy thermometer to side of pan, making sure bulb is completely submerged in sugar mixture but not touching bottom of pan.

4. Continue heating, *without stirring*, until mixture reaches soft-ball stage (234°F) on candy thermometer.

5. Remove from heat and add vanilla milk chips. Stir with wooden spoon until melted. Add marshmallow creme, walnuts and vanilla, stirring well after each addition.

6. Pour into prepared pan. Score into squares by cutting halfway through fudge with sharp knife while fudge is still warm.

7. Remove from pan by lifting fudge and foil using foil handles. Place on cutting board. Cool completely. Cut along score lines into squares. Remove foil.   *Makes about 3 pounds*

Step 1. Lining pan with foil.

Step 3. Attaching candy thermometer to pan.

Step 7. Lifting fudge from pan.

Simple Spumoni

2 cups whipping cream
⅔ cup (7 ounces) sweetened condensed milk
½ teaspoon rum extract
1 can (21 ounces) cherry pie filling
½ cup chopped almonds
½ cup miniature chocolate chips
Slivered almonds and cookies for garnish

1. Combine whipping cream, sweetened condensed milk and rum extract in large bowl; refrigerate 30 minutes.

2. Remove cream mixture from refrigerator and beat just until soft peaks form. To test, lift beaters; mixture should form droopy, but definite, peaks. *Do not overbeat.*

3. Fold in cherry pie filling with rubber spatula by gently cutting down to bottom of bowl, scraping up side of bowl, then folding over top of mixture. Repeat until filling is evenly incorporated.

4. Fold in chopped almonds and chocolate chips as described in step 3.

5. Transfer to 8-inch square pan. Cover and freeze about 4 hours or until firm.

6. Scoop out to serve. Garnish, if desired.

Makes about 1 quart

Step 3. Folding cherry pie filling into cream mixture.

Step 5. Transferring mixture to pan.

Step 6. Scooping out to serve.

Chocolate Rice Pudding

2 cups water
1 cup uncooked Uncle Ben's®
   Converted® Brand Rice
2 tablespoons butter
¼ cup sugar
2 teaspoons cornstarch
2 cups milk
½ teaspoon vanilla
2 egg yolks (technique on
   page 17)
½ cup semisweet chocolate chips
   Sweetened Whipped Cream
   (page 16), unsweetened cocoa
   powder and cookies for
   garnish

1. Bring water to a boil in large saucepan. Stir in rice and butter. Reduce heat; cover and simmer 20 minutes. Remove from heat. Let stand covered until all liquid is absorbed, about 5 minutes.

2. Combine sugar and cornstarch in small bowl; add to hot rice in saucepan. Stir in milk.

3. Bring mixture to a boil, stirring occasionally. Boil 1 minute, stirring constantly. Remove from heat; stir in vanilla.

4. Beat egg yolks in small bowl. Stir about 1 cup of hot rice mixture into beaten egg yolks.

5. Stir egg yolk mixture back into remaining rice mixture in saucepan.

6. Cook rice mixture over medium heat, stirring frequently, just until mixture starts to bubble. Remove from heat; add chocolate chips and stir until melted.

7. Spoon into individual serving dishes. Refrigerate.

8. Prepare Sweetened Whipped Cream. Spoon into pastry bag fitted with large star decorator tip. Pipe onto top of each serving.

9. Sift unsweetened cocoa powder through fine-meshed strainer or sifter over each serving. Garnish, if desired.

Makes 6 servings

Step 4. Adding hot rice mixture to egg yolks.

Step 5. Adding egg yolk mixture back to rice mixture.

Step 8. Piping Sweetened Whipped Cream onto each serving.

Chocolate Chiffon Cake

1 cup all-purpose flour
1 teaspoon baking powder
½ teaspoon salt
1 bar (4 ounces) German's sweet
    baking chocolate
½ cup hot water
5 eggs, separated (technique on
    page 17)
⅔ cup granulated sugar
1 teaspoon vanilla
    Powdered sugar

1. Preheat oven to 350°F.

2. Combine flour, baking powder and salt in small bowl; set aside.

3. Combine chocolate and hot water in small, heavy saucepan. Melt chocolate over low heat, stirring occasionally; set aside.

4. Beat egg whites in clean large bowl with electric mixer at high speed until foamy. Gradually beat in sugar until stiff peaks form; set aside.

5. Combine melted chocolate mixture, egg yolks and vanilla in large bowl. Beat with electric mixer at low speed until well blended, scraping down side of bowl once.

6. Gradually add flour mixture to chocolate mixture. Beat with electric mixer at low speed until well blended.

7. Fold chocolate mixture into egg white mixture. (Technique on page 44.)

8. Pour into ungreased 10-inch tube pan. Run long metal spatula through batter to break up any large air bubbles.

9. Bake 45 to 50 minutes or until top springs back when lightly touched with finger.

10. Invert cake in pan onto heatproof bottle or funnel. Cool completely.

11. Remove from pan. Sift powdered sugar through fine-meshed sieve or sifter onto top of cake.   *Makes about 12 servings*

Step 4. Testing for stiff peaks.

Step 8. Running spatula through batter.

Step 10. Inverting cake in pan onto bottle to cool.

Orange Cappuccino Brownies

¾ cup butter
2 squares (1 ounce each) semisweet chocolate, coarsely chopped
2 squares (1 ounce each) unsweetened chocolate, coarsely chopped
1¾ cups granulated sugar
1 tablespoon instant espresso powder or instant coffee granules
3 eggs
¼ cup orange-flavored liqueur
2 teaspoons grated orange peel (technique on page 35)
1 cup all-purpose flour
1 package (12 ounces) semisweet chocolate chips
2 tablespoons shortening
1 orange for garnish

1. Preheat oven to 350°F. Grease 13 × 9-inch baking pan.

2. Melt butter, chopped semisweet chocolate and unsweetened chocolate in large heavy saucepan over low heat, stirring constantly. Stir in granulated sugar and espresso powder. Remove from heat. Cool slightly.

3. Beat in eggs, 1 at a time, with wire whisk. Whisk in liqueur and orange peel.

4. Beat flour into chocolate mixture until just blended. Spread batter evenly into prepared baking pan.

5. Bake 25 to 30 minutes or until center is just set. Remove pan to wire rack.

6. Meanwhile, melt chocolate chips and shortening in small, heavy saucepan over low heat, stirring constantly.

7. Immediately after removing brownies from oven, spread hot chocolate mixture over warm brownies. Cool completely in pan on wire rack. Cut into 2-inch squares.

8. To make orange peel garnish, remove thin strips of peel from orange using citrus zester.

9. Tie strips into knots or twist into spirals. Garnish, if desired.

Makes about 2 dozen brownies

Step 4. Spreading batter into prepared pan.

Step 7. Spreading hot chocolate mixture over warm brownies.

Step 8. Removing thin strips of orange peel for garnish.

Raspberry Chocolate Mousse Pie

40 chocolate wafer cookies
¼ cup butter, melted
6 squares (1 ounce each) semisweet chocolate
1¼ cups whipping cream
½ cup water
7 tablespoons sugar
5 egg yolks (technique on page 17)
3 tablespoons raspberry-flavored liqueur
Sweetened Whipped Cream (page 16), fresh raspberries and mint leaves for garnish

1. Place cookies in food processor or blender container; process with on/off pulses until finely crushed.

2. Combine cookie crumbs and butter in medium bowl; mix well. Press firmly onto bottom and 1 inch up side of 9-inch springform pan.

3. Melt chocolate in top of double boiler over hot, not boiling, water. Cool slightly.

4. Beat whipping cream with electric mixer at high speed until soft peaks form. (Technique on page 56.) Refrigerate.

5. Combine water and sugar in small saucepan. Bring to a boil over medium-high heat. Boil 1 minute. Place hot syrup in 1-cup glass measure.

6. Place egg yolks in large, deep, heatproof bowl. Whisk in hot syrup. Place bowl in large saucepan of hot, not boiling, water. Continue to whisk until soft peaks form. To test, lift whisk; mixture should form droopy, but definite, peaks. Remove from heat.

7. Beat mixture until cool. Stir in melted chocolate and liqueur.

8. Stir ½ cup whipped cream into chocolate mixture.

9. Fold in remaining whipped cream. (Technique on page 44.)

10. Pour into prepared crust. Refrigerate until firm, about 3 hours or overnight.

11. To serve, remove side of pan. Garnish, if desired. *Makes 10 servings*

Step 1. Processing cookies in food processor.

Step 2. Pressing crumb mixture onto bottom and 1 inch up side of pan.

Step 6. Whisking hot syrup into egg yolks.

Almond Chocolate Crown

2 packages (3 ounces each) ladyfingers
4 eggs*
1 cup milk
1 envelope unflavored gelatin
1 cup sugar, divided
⅔ cup unsweetened cocoa powder
¼ cup almond-flavored liqueur
1½ cups whipping cream
Almond Cream (page 56)
Sliced almonds for garnish

*Use clean, uncracked eggs.

1. Gently split ladyfingers using serrated knife. Line bottom and side of 9-inch springform pan with split ladyfingers, cut side facing in. Refrigerate.

2. To separate egg yolk from white, gently tap egg in center against hard surface, such as side of bowl. Holding shell half in each hand, gently transfer yolk back and forth between the 2 shell halves. Allow white to drip down between the 2 halves into bowl.

3. When all the white has dripped into bowl, place yolk in another bowl. Transfer white to third bowl. Repeat with remaining 3 eggs. (Egg whites must be free from any egg yolk to reach the proper volume when beaten.)

4. Combine egg yolks and milk in small bowl; beat well.

5. Combine gelatin, ³/₄ cup sugar and cocoa in medium saucepan.

6. Add egg yolk mixture to gelatin mixture. Let stand, without stirring, 3 minutes for gelatin to soften.

7. Heat over low heat, stirring constantly, until gelatin is completely dissolved, about 5 minutes. To test for undissolved gelatin, run a finger over the spoon. If it is smooth, the gelatin is completely dissolved; if it feels granular, continue heating until it feels smooth.

continued on page 56

Step 1. Lining pan with ladyfingers.

Step 2. Separating egg yolk from white.

Step 7. Testing for undissolved gelatin.

8. Remove from heat. Using wire whisk, beat until completely blended. Whisk in liqueur.

9. Pour mixture into large bowl. Place bowl in refrigerator; stir mixture occasionally. Chill until mixture mounds slightly when dropped from spoon. (Technique on page 57.) Remove from refrigerator.

10. Chill large bowl and beaters thoroughly. Pour chilled whipping cream into chilled bowl and beat with electric mixer at high speed until soft peaks form. To test, lift beaters from whipping cream; mixture should form droopy, but definite, peaks. Refrigerate.

11. Clean beaters thoroughly. Beat egg whites in separate clean large bowl with electric mixer at high speed until foamy. Gradually beat in remaining 1/4 cup sugar until stiff peaks form; set aside.

12. Fold gelatin mixture into egg white mixture with rubber spatula by gently cutting down to bottom of bowl, scraping up side of bowl, then folding over top of mixture. Repeat until gelatin mixture is evenly incorporated into egg white mixture.

13. Fold whipped cream into egg white mixture as described in step 12. Pour mixture into ladyfinger-lined pan. Refrigerate 4 hours or overnight until firm.

14. Prepare Almond Cream. To serve, remove side of pan. Cut into serving pieces. Serve with Almond Cream. Garnish, if desired.

Makes about 12 servings

Almond Cream

½ **cup whipping cream**
1 **tablespoon powdered sugar**
1 **tablespoon almond-flavored liqueur**

1. Chill small bowl and beaters thoroughly. Pour chilled whipping cream into chilled bowl and beat with electric mixer at high speed until thickened. Add powdered sugar and beat until soft peaks form. To test, lift beaters from whipping cream; mixture should form droopy, but definite, peaks.

2. Fold in almond-flavored liqueur as described in step 12 of main recipe.

Makes about 1 cup

Step 11. Testing for stiff peaks.

Step 12. Folding gelatin mixture into egg white mixture.

Almond Cream: Step 1. Beating whipping cream until soft peaks form.

Black Forest Soufflé

3 eggs*
2 cups milk
2 envelopes unflavored gelatin
¾ cup sugar, divided
4 squares (1 ounce each)
    semisweet chocolate, chopped
2 teaspoons rum extract
1½ teaspoons vanilla
2 cups whipping cream, divided
1 can (21 ounces) cherry pie
    filling
⅓ cup chopped almonds
    Chocolate Curls (page 58) for
    garnish
    Maraschino cherries for
    garnish

*Use clean, uncracked eggs.

1. Cut 18 × 16-inch piece of waxed paper. Fold lengthwise in half. Grease and flour. Wrap waxed paper around rim of 1½-quart soufflé dish, greased side in, forming a "collar." Tape to secure in place.

2. Separate egg yolks from whites. (Technique on page 17.)

3. Combine egg yolks and milk in small bowl; beat until well combined.

4. Combine gelatin and ½ cup sugar in medium saucepan. Add egg yolk mixture to gelatin mixture. Let stand, without stirring, 3 minutes for gelatin to soften.

5. Heat over low heat, stirring constantly, until gelatin is completely dissolved, about 5 minutes. To test for undissolved gelatin, run a finger over the spoon. If it is smooth, the gelatin is completely dissolved; if it feels granular, continue heating until it feels smooth.

6. Add chopped chocolate to dissolved gelatin mixture; stir until completely melted. Beat with wire whisk until thoroughly blended. Stir in rum extract and vanilla.

7. Pour mixture into large bowl. Place bowl in refrigerator; stir mixture occasionally. Chill until mixture mounds slightly when dropped from spoon. Remove from refrigerator.

continued on page 58

Step 1. Taping "collar" in place.

Step 5. Testing for undissolved gelatin.

Step 7. Testing gelatin mixture.

Black Forest Soufflé, *continued*

8. To make meringue, beat egg whites in clean large bowl with electric mixer at high speed until foamy. Gradually beat in remaining 1/4 cup sugar until stiff peaks form. After beaters are lifted from meringue, stiff peaks should remain on surface, and mixture will not slide around when bowl is tilted.

9. Fold meringue into chocolate-gelatin mixture with rubber spatula by gently cutting down to bottom of bowl, scraping up side of bowl, then folding over top of mixture. Repeat until egg whites are evenly incorporated into chocolate-gelatin mixture.

10. Chill large bowl and beaters thoroughly. Pour chilled whipping cream into chilled bowl and beat with electric mixer at high speed until soft peaks form. To test, lift beaters from whipping cream; mixture should form droopy, but definite, peaks.

11. Fold 3 cups whipped cream into chocolate-gelatin mixture as described in step 9. Reserve remaining whipped cream for garnish.

12. Fold cherry pie filling and almonds into chocolate mixture as described in step 9.

13. Pour mixture into prepared dish; refrigerate until set.

14. Prepare Chocolate Curls. To serve, remove collar. Garnish, if desired.

Makes about 10 servings

Chocolate Curls

2 squares (1 ounce each) semisweet chocolate

1. Allow chocolate to soften by setting in warm place for 30 minutes. Chocolate should still be firm.

2. Make chocolate curls using vegetable peeler.

3. Carefully pick up each chocolate curl by inserting a wooden toothpick in center. Lift to waxed paper-lined baking sheet. Refrigerate about 15 minutes until firm.

Step 9. Folding meringue into chocolate-gelatin mixture.

Step 10. Beating whipping cream until soft peaks form.

Chocolate Curls: Step 2. Making chocolate curls using vegetable peeler.

Double Chocolate Bombe

5 eggs, divided*
1½ cups whipping cream, divided
    Chocolate Cake (page 63)
1 envelope unflavored gelatin
1 package (12 ounces) semisweet
    chocolate chips
¼ teaspoon salt
⅓ cup sugar
    White Chocolate Cutouts
    (page 63) for garnish
1 white chocolate baking bar
    (2 ounces) for drizzling

*Use clean, uncracked eggs.

1. Line 2-quart bowl with plastic wrap; oil lightly.

2. To separate egg white from yolk, gently tap egg in center against hard surface, such as side of bowl. Holding shell half in each hand, gently transfer yolk back and forth between the 2 shell halves. Allow white to drip down between the 2 halves into bowl.

3. When all white has dripped into bowl, place yolk in another bowl. Transfer white to third bowl. Repeat with remaining 4 eggs. (Egg whites must be free from any egg yolk to reach the proper volume when beaten.)

4. Place egg yolks and ½ cup whipping cream in small bowl; beat slightly with fork. Sprinkle gelatin over egg yolk mixture. Let stand without stirring 5 minutes to soften.

5. Melt chocolate chips in top of double boiler over hot, not boiling, water.

6. Stir about ½ cup melted chocolate into egg yolk mixture.

7. Stir egg yolk mixture back into remaining chocolate in top of double boiler. Continue to heat until gelatin is completely dissolved. (Technique on page 23.)

continued on page 62

Step 1. Oiling lined bowl.

Step 2. Separating egg white from yolk.

Step 7. Stirring egg yolk mixture back into chocolate.

Double Chocolate Bombe, continued

8. To make meringue, beat egg whites and salt in clean large bowl with electric mixer at high speed until foamy. Gradually beat in sugar until stiff peaks form. After beaters are lifted from meringue, stiff peaks should remain on surface, and mixture will not slide around when bowl is tilted.

9. Fold in chocolate mixture with rubber spatula by gently cutting down to bottom of bowl, scraping up side of bowl, then folding over top of mixture. Repeat until chocolate mixture is evenly incorporated into meringue.

10. Beat remaining 1 cup whipping cream until soft peaks form. (Technique on page 56.)

11. Fold into chocolate mixture as described in step 9.

12. Pour into prepared bowl. Cover and refrigerate 4 hours.

13. Prepare Chocolate Cake and White Chocolate Cutouts.

14. Place cake on serving plate. Unmold mousse onto cake. Remove plastic wrap. Trim edge of cake around mousse, if desired.

15. Place white chocolate baking bar in small resealable plastic freezer bag. Microwave at MEDIUM (50% power) 2 minutes. Turn bag over; microwave at MEDIUM (50% power) 2 to 3 minutes or until chocolate is melted. Knead bag until chocolate is smooth.

16. Cut off very tiny corner of bag; drizzle white chocolate over mousse. Refrigerate until white chocolate is set, about 30 minutes. Garnish, if desired.

Makes about 8 servings

Step 8. Testing for stiff peaks.

Step 14. Removing plastic wrap.

Step 16. Drizzling white chocolate over mousse.

Chocolate Cake

1 cup sugar
⅓ cup shortening
2 eggs
⅓ cup water
½ teaspoon vanilla
1 cup all-purpose flour
⅓ cup unsweetened cocoa powder
1 teaspoon baking soda
¼ teaspoon baking powder
¼ teaspoon salt

1. Preheat oven to 375°F. Grease bottom and side of 9-inch round baking pan. Add 2 to 3 teaspoons flour to pan. Gently tap side of pan to evenly coat bottom and side with flour. (Technique on page 32.)

2. Combine sugar and shortening in large bowl. Beat with electric mixer at medium speed until light and fluffy, scraping down side of bowl once. Add eggs, water and vanilla; beat well.

3. Combine flour, cocoa, baking soda, baking powder and salt in small bowl. Add to shortening mixture; beat with electric mixer at medium speed until smooth. Pour batter into prepared pan.

4. Bake 20 to 25 minutes or until cake tester or wooden pick inserted into center comes out clean. Cool 10 minutes in pan.

5. Loosen edge and remove to wire rack; cool completely.

White Chocolate Cutouts

2 white chocolate baking bars
(2 ounces each), coarsely chopped

1. Melt chocolate in small bowl set in bowl of very hot water, stirring occasionally. This will take about 10 minutes.

2. Spread onto waxed paper-lined cookie sheet. Refrigerate until firm, about 15 minutes.

3. Cut into large triangle shapes with sharp knife.

4. Immediately lift shapes carefully from waxed paper with spatula or knife. Refrigerate until ready to use.

White Chocolate Cutouts:
Step 1. Melting white chocolate.

White Chocolate Cutouts:
Step 2. Spreading white chocolate onto cookie sheet.

White Chocolate Cutouts:
Step 3. Cutting into shapes.

Apples 'n' Honey Nut Tart

1¼ cups all-purpose flour
⅓ cup wheat germ
⅓ cup packed brown sugar
½ teaspoon salt
¾ teaspoon grated orange peel, divided (technique on page 35)
½ cup cold butter, cut into pieces
1 egg, beaten
1 cup coarsely chopped pecans
⅓ cup golden raisins
2½ pounds apples
8 tablespoons honey, divided
2 tablespoons butter, melted
½ teaspoon ground cinnamon
⅓ cup orange marmalade
⅔ cup whipping cream

1. Combine flour, wheat germ, brown sugar, salt and ½ teaspoon grated orange peel in large bowl. Cut in cold butter with pastry blender or 2 knives until mixture forms pea-sized pieces. Add egg; stir until well blended.

2. Press firmly onto bottom and up side of 9-inch tart pan with removable bottom. Freeze until very firm, about 30 minutes.

3. Preheat oven to 350°F.

4. Combine pecans and raisins in small bowl. Sprinkle on bottom of chilled crust.

5. Peel apples. For center slice, place peeled apple, with stem facing away from you, on cutting board. Cut a ¼-inch-thick slice from center of apple. Place in center of tart.

6. Remove cores from remaining apples; discard. Cut apples into ¼-inch-thick slices.

7. Combine 6 tablespoons honey, melted butter, remaining ¼ teaspoon orange peel, cinnamon and apple slices in large bowl; stir to coat apples.

8. Arrange apple slices in circular pattern on top of pecans and raisins. Drizzle any honey mixture left in bowl over apples. Bake 50 to 55 minutes or until apples are tender.

9. Place marmalade in small saucepan. Heat over medium heat until warm, stirring occasionally. Brush over apples. Cool; remove side of tart pan.

10. Beat whipping cream and remaining 2 tablespoons honey until soft peaks form. (Technique on page 56.) Serve tart with whipped cream.   *Makes 8 to 10 servings*

Step 5. Cutting slice from center of apple.

Step 6. Cutting apples into slices.

Step 9. Brushing marmalade over apples.

Pineapple Macadamia Cheesepie

**Macadamia Nut Crust
(recipe follows)**
12 ounces cream cheese
**1 can (8 ounces) Dole® Crushed
Pineapple in Juice**
1 egg
¾ cup plain yogurt
½ cup sugar
1 teaspoon vanilla
**Macadamia nuts and pineapple
leaves for garnish**

1. Preheat oven to 350°F. Prepare Macadamia Nut Crust.

2. Place cream cheese on opened packages on cutting board. With utility knife, cut cream cheese into ¹/₂-inch pieces. Let stand at room temperature until softened. (Cream cheese will be easy to push down.)

3. Drain pineapple, pressing out excess juice with back of spoon. Reserve 2 tablespoons pineapple. Spread remaining pineapple over prepared crust.

4. Combine cream cheese, egg, yogurt, sugar and vanilla in medium bowl; blend thoroughly. Pour over pineapple in crust.

5. Bake 20 minutes or until just set; cool completely on wire rack. Refrigerate.

6. Before serving, garnish with reserved 2 tablespoons pineapple, additional macadamia nuts and pineapple leaves.

Makes 6 servings

Macadamia Nut Crust

12 graham cracker squares
1 cup macadamia nuts
6 tablespoons butter, melted
2 tablespoons sugar

1. Process graham crackers and macadamia nuts in food processor until finely crushed. Measure 1³/₄ cups.

2. Combine crumb mixture, butter and sugar in small bowl.

3. Press firmly onto bottom and up side of

Step 2. Softening cream cheese.

Step 4. Pouring cream cheese mixture over pineapple in crust.

Macadamia Nut Crust: Step 1. Processing crackers and nuts until finely crushed.

Ginger & Pear Tart

30 gingersnap cookies
½ cup chopped pecans
⅓ cup butter, melted
1 cup sour cream
¾ cup half-and-half
1 package (4-serving size) vanilla
   instant pudding mix
2 tablespoons apricot brandy
4 ripe pears*
⅓ cup packed dark brown sugar
½ teaspoon ground ginger

*Or, substitute 1 (16-ounce) can pear halves, drained and thinly sliced, for fresh pears.

1. Preheat oven to 350°F.

2. Combine cookies and pecans in food processor or blender container; process with on/off pulses until finely crushed. (Technique on page 14.)

3. Combine crumb mixture and butter in medium bowl. Press firmly onto bottom and up side of 10-inch quiche dish or 9-inch pie plate. Bake 7 minutes; cool completely on wire rack.

4. Combine sour cream and half-and-half in large bowl. Beat until smooth. Whisk in pudding mix. Add apricot brandy. Beat until smooth.

5. Pour into prepared crust. Cover; refrigerate several hours or overnight.

6. Just before serving, preheat broiler. Peel pears with vegetable peeler. Cut pears in half lengthwise. Remove cores and seeds; discard. Cut pears into thin slices.

7. Arrange pear slices in overlapping circles on top of pudding mixture.

8. Combine brown sugar and ginger in small bowl. Sprinkle evenly over pears. Broil 4 to 6 minutes or until sugar is melted and bubbly. Watch carefully so sugar does not burn. Serve immediately.   *Makes 6 to 8 servings*

Step 3. Pressing crumb mixture into quiche dish.

Step 6. Cutting pears into thin slices.

Step 7. Arranging pear slices on top of pudding mixture.

Crunchy Peach Cobbler

1 can (29 ounces) *or* 2 cans
  (16 ounces each) cling peach
  slices in syrup
⅓ cup *plus* 1 tablespoon
  granulated sugar, divided
1 tablespoon cornstarch
½ teaspoon vanilla
½ cup packed brown sugar
2 cups all-purpose flour, divided
⅓ cup uncooked rolled oats
¼ cup margarine or butter, melted
½ teaspoon ground cinnamon
½ teaspoon salt
½ cup shortening
4 to 5 tablespoons cold water
  Sweetened Whipped Cream
  (page 16) for garnish

1. Drain peach slices in fine-meshed sieve over 2-cup glass measure. Reserve ³/₄ cup syrup.

2. Combine ¹/₃ cup granulated sugar and cornstarch in small saucepan. Slowly add reserved syrup. Stir well. Add vanilla. Cook over low heat, stirring constantly, until thickened. Set aside.

3. Combine brown sugar, ¹/₂ cup flour, oats, margarine and cinnamon in small bowl; stir until mixture forms coarse crumbs. Set aside.

4. Preheat oven to 350°F.

5. Combine remaining 1¹/₂ cups flour, 1 tablespoon granulated sugar and salt in small bowl. Cut in shortening with pastry blender or 2 knives until mixture forms pea-sized pieces.

6. Sprinkle water, 1 tablespoon at a time, over flour mixture. Toss lightly with fork until mixture holds together. Press together to form a ball.

7. Roll out dough into square ¹/₈ inch thick, following steps 3 and 4 on page 28. Cut into 10-inch square.

8. Fold dough in half, then in half again. Carefully place folded dough in center of 8 × 8-inch baking dish. Unfold and press onto bottom and about 1 inch up sides of dish.

9. Arrange peaches over crust. Pour sauce over peaches. Sprinkle with crumb topping.

10. Bake 45 minutes. Prepare Sweetened Whipped Cream. Serve warm or at room temperature with Sweetened Whipped Cream.

Makes about 6 servings

Step 1. Draining peaches.

Step 5. Cutting in shortening until mixture forms pea-sized pieces.

Step 8. Pressing dough onto bottom and up sides of dish.

Raspberry Cheesecake Blossoms

3 packages (10 ounces each) frozen raspberries, thawed
¼ cup butter, melted
8 sheets phyllo dough*
1 package (8 ounces) cream cheese, softened (technique on page 14)
½ cup cottage cheese
1 egg
½ cup *plus* 3 tablespoons sugar, divided
4 teaspoons lemon juice, divided
½ teaspoon vanilla
Fresh raspberries and sliced kiwifruit for garnish

*Cover with plastic wrap, then a damp kitchen towel to prevent dough from drying out.

1. Drain thawed raspberries in fine-meshed sieve over 1-cup glass measure. Reserve syrup.

2. Preheat oven to 350°F. Grease 12 (2½-inch) muffin cups.

3. Brush melted butter onto 1 phyllo sheet. Cover with second phyllo sheet; brush with butter. Repeat with remaining sheets of phyllo.

4. Cut stack of phyllo dough in half lengthwise and then in thirds crosswise, to make a total of 12 squares. Gently fit each stacked square into prepared muffin cup.

5. Place cream cheese, cottage cheese, egg, 3 tablespoons sugar, 1 teaspoon lemon juice and vanilla in food processor or blender. Process until smooth. Divide mixture evenly among muffin cups.

6. Bake 10 to 15 minutes or until lightly browned. Carefully remove from muffin cups to wire racks to cool.

7. Bring reserved raspberry syrup to a boil in small saucepan over medium-high heat. Cook until reduced to ¾ cup, stirring occasionally.

8. Place thawed raspberries in food processor or blender. Process until smooth. Press through fine-meshed sieve with back of spoon to remove seeds.

9. Combine raspberry puree, reduced syrup, remaining ½ cup sugar and 3 teaspoons lemon juice in small bowl. Mix well.

10. To serve, spoon raspberry sauce onto 12 dessert plates. Place cheesecake blossom on each plate. Garnish, if desired.

Makes 12 servings

Step 1. Draining raspberries.

Step 3. Brushing butter onto phyllo.

Step 4. Fitting phyllo dough into muffin cups.

Apricot Roll-Ups

4 cups dried apricots
1 can (12 ounces) apricot-
    pineapple nectar
1½ cups water
½ cup sugar
2 tablespoons lemon juice
1 tablespoon quick-cooking
    tapioca
2 cups finely chopped walnuts
1 package (7 ounces) shredded
    coconut
1 package egg roll wrappers
    Vegetable oil for frying
    Sour cream and chocolate
    sauce for dipping

1. Combine apricots, nectar, water, sugar and lemon juice in large saucepan; bring to a boil. Remove from heat; cover and let stand 1 hour.

2. Drain, reserving liquid. Finely chop apricots. Combine apricots, reserved liquid and tapioca in same saucepan; bring to a boil, stirring constantly. Remove from heat and let stand 20 minutes. Stir in walnuts and coconut.

3. For each roll-up, place egg roll wrapper point toward edge of counter. Spoon about 2 heaping tablespoons of apricot mixture across and just below center of wrapper.

4. Fold bottom point of wrapper up over filling. Fold side points over filling, forming an envelope shape. Moisten inside edges of top point with water and roll toward that point, pressing firmly to seal. Repeat with remaining wrappers and filling.

5. Pour 2 inches oil into heavy saucepan. Attach deep-fry thermometer to side of pan, making sure bulb is completely submerged in oil but not touching bottom of pan. Heat oil over medium heat to 370°F. Add roll-ups to oil, a few at a time, seam side down. Fry 2 to 4 minutes or until golden brown, turning once or twice.

6. Remove with tongs; drain on paper towels. Serve with sour cream and chocolate sauce for dipping. *Makes 20 to 26 roll-ups*

Step 3. Spooning apricot mixture onto wrapper.

Step 4. Moistening edges of wrapper with water.

Step 5. Frying roll-ups until golden brown.

Fabulous Fruit & Cheese Tart

1 cup all-purpose flour
½ cup *plus* 3 tablespoons sugar, divided
6 tablespoons cold butter
1 egg yolk (technique on page 17)
3 tablespoons water, divided
½ teaspoon almond extract
    Pinch salt
½ cup apple or currant jelly
1 pound Polly-O® Ricotta Cheese
1 package (3 ounces) cream cheese, softened (technique on page 14)
3 tablespoons orange-flavored liqueur
1 pint strawberries
2 kiwifruit

1. Combine flour and 3 tablespoons sugar in large bowl. Cut in butter using pastry blender or 2 knives until mixture forms pea-sized pieces.

2. Add egg yolk, 1 tablespoon water, almond extract and salt; toss with fork until mixture holds together. Press dough to form a ball. Refrigerate 30 minutes.

3. Preheat oven to 400°F.

4. Press dough between hands to form a 5- to 6-inch disk. Lightly flour surface and rolling pin. Roll dough in short strokes starting in middle of disk and rolling out toward edge. Rotate dough ¼ turn to the right. Sprinkle more flour under dough and on rolling pin as necessary to prevent sticking. Continue to roll and rotate dough 2 to 3 more times.

5. Roll out dough into ⅛-inch-thick circle at least 1 inch larger than inverted tart pan. Place rolling pin on one side of dough. Gently roll dough over rolling pin once.

6. Carefully lift rolling pin and dough, unrolling dough over tart pan. Ease dough into tart pan with fingertips. Do not stretch dough. Cut dough even with edge of tart pan.

continued on page 78

Step 1. Cutting in butter until mixture forms pea-sized pieces.

Step 5. Rolling out dough into circle.

Step 6. Cutting dough even with edge of tart pan.

Fabulous Fruit & Cheese Tart, continued

7. Cover crust with plastic wrap and refrigerate 30 minutes to allow dough to relax.

8. Pierce bottom and sides of crust with fork at ¼-inch intervals, about 40 times.

9. Cut square of foil about 4 inches larger than tart pan. Line crust with foil. Fill with dried beans, uncooked rice or ceramic pie weights.

10. Bake 10 minutes or until set. Remove from oven. Gently remove foil lining and beans. Return to oven and bake 5 minutes or until very light brown. Cool completely on wire rack.

11. Place jelly and remaining 2 tablespoons water in small saucepan. Melt over medium-low heat, stirring constantly. Brush on cooled crust.

12. Combine ricotta cheese, cream cheese, remaining ½ cup sugar and liqueur in large bowl. Beat with electric mixer at high speed until smooth, scraping down side of bowl once. Spread over glazed crust.

13. Cut green tops off strawberries with utility knife. Cut each strawberry in half.

14. Peel kiwifruit with vegetable peeler. Cut into slices with utility knife.

15. Arrange strawberry halves and kiwi slices in circles on top of tart. Refrigerate 2 hours.   *Makes 6 servings*

Step 8. Piercing crust with fork.

Step 9. Filling lined crust with dried beans.

Step 13. Cutting strawberries into halves.

The Golden Strawberry

1 pint strawberries
1 envelope Knox® Unflavored
Gelatine
⅓ cup strawberry-flavored liqueur
6 ounces Montrachet goat
cheese*
4 tablespoons sugar, divided
¼ cup sour cream
2 tablespoons honey
½ teaspoon ground cinnamon
¼ teaspoon ground nutmeg
3 eggs**
½ cup whipping cream
6 ounces amaretti cookies
Whipped cream, additional
strawberries and amaretti
cookies for garnish

*Montrachet cheese is a white chevre from France. It has a soft, moist, creamy texture and a mildly tangy flavor. It can be found in the gourmet or imported cheese section of most supermarkets or specialty food stores.

**Use clean, uncracked eggs.

1. Cut green tops off strawberries with utility knife. Cut each strawberry into quarters.

2. Sprinkle gelatine over liqueur in small saucepan. Let stand without stirring 3 minutes for gelatine to soften.

3. Heat over low heat, stirring constantly, until gelatine is completely dissolved, about 5 minutes. To test for undissolved gelatine, run a finger over the spoon. If it is smooth, the gelatine is completely dissolved; if it feels granular, continue heating until it feels smooth.

4. Using wire whisk, blend cheese and 2 tablespoons sugar into dissolved gelatine mixture; pour into large bowl. Add sour cream, honey, cinnamon and nutmeg; mix well. Set aside.

5. To separate egg white from yolk, gently tap egg in center against hard surface, such as side of bowl. Holding shell half in each hand, gently transfer yolk back and forth between the 2 shell halves. Allow white to drip down between 2 halves into bowl.

continued on page 80

Step 1. Cutting strawberries into quarters.

Step 3. Testing for undissolved gelatine.

Step 5. Separating egg white from yolk.

The Golden Strawberry, continued

6. When all the white has dripped into bowl, place yolk in another bowl. Transfer white to third bowl. Repeat with remaining 2 eggs. (Egg whites must be free from any egg yolk to reach the proper volume when beaten.) Store unused egg yolks, covered with water, in an airtight container. Refrigerate for 2 or 3 days.

7. Beat egg whites in clean large bowl with electric mixer at high speed until foamy. Gradually beat in remaining 2 tablespoons sugar until stiff peaks form. (After beaters are lifted from meringue, stiff peaks should remain on surface, and mixture will not slide around when bowl is tilted.)

8. Fold egg white mixture into gelatine mixture with rubber spatula by gently cutting down to bottom of bowl, scraping up side of bowl, then folding over top of mixture. Repeat until egg white mixture is evenly incorporated into gelatine mixture.

9. Chill small bowl and beaters thoroughly. Pour chilled whipping cream into chilled bowl and beat with electric mixer at high speed until soft peaks form. To test, lift beaters from whipping cream; mixture should form droopy, but definite, peaks.

10. Fold whipped cream and quartered strawberries into gelatine mixture as described in step 8.

11. Place cookies in resealable plastic bag. Squeeze out excess air; seal bag tightly. Roll over cookies with rolling pin until crushed.

12. Alternately layer strawberry mixture and crushed cookies in parfait glasses or dessert dishes; refrigerate until completely set. Garnish, if desired.

Makes 8 servings

Step 7. Testing for stiff peaks.

Step 11. Crushing cookies.

Step 12. Layering strawberry mixture and cookies in parfait glasses.

Acini di Pepe Fruit Pudding

1 cup acini di pepe or other small pasta
1 can (20 ounces) crushed pineapple in juice, undrained
¾ cup milk
2 eggs, well beaten
½ cup granulated sugar
½ teaspoon grated lemon peel (technique on page 17)
½ teaspoon ground cinnamon (optional)
⅔ cup packed brown sugar
⅔ cup finely chopped walnuts
¼ cup all-purpose flour
6 tablespoons cold butter or margarine
Sweetened Whipped Cream (page 16)

1. Cook acini di pepe according to package directions; drain well.

2. Preheat oven to 375°F. Grease 8-inch baking pan.

3. Drain pineapple in fine-meshed sieve over 1-cup glass measure. Reserve ½ cup juice.

4. Combine reserved ½ cup juice, cooked pasta, milk, eggs, granulated sugar, grated lemon peel and cinnamon in large bowl; mix well. Spoon mixture into prepared pan. Top with crushed pineapple.

5. Combine brown sugar, walnuts and flour in small bowl; cut in butter with pastry blender or 2 knives until mixture forms pea-sized pieces. Sprinkle evenly over pineapple.

6. Bake 60 minutes or until knife inserted into center comes out clean.

7. Prepare Sweetened Whipped Cream.

8. Spoon into serving dishes and serve warm or cold with Sweetened Whipped Cream.

Makes 8 servings

Note: Any type of canned fruit pieces in fruit juice may be used, such as peaches, pears, fruit cocktail, etc.

Step 3. Draining pineapple.

Step 5. Cutting in butter until mixture forms pea-sized pieces.

Step 6. Testing for doneness.

Coconut Cheesecake

1 can (3½ ounces) flaked coconut
  (1⅓ cups), divided
20 chocolate wafer cookies
1 cup finely chopped pecans
2 tablespoons sugar
¼ cup margarine or butter, melted
3 packages (8 ounces each)
  cream cheese, softened
  (technique on page 14)
3 eggs
2 tablespoons all-purpose flour
1 can (15 ounces) Coco Lopez®
  Cream of Coconut
  Sweetened Whipped Cream
  (page 16) for garnish

1. Preheat oven to 300°F.

2. To toast coconut, spread on baking sheet. Bake 4 to 6 minutes or until light golden brown, stirring frequently. Remove coconut from baking sheet and cool; set aside.

3. Place cookies in food processor or blender; process with on/off pulses until finely crushed.

4. Combine cookie crumbs, pecans and sugar in small bowl; stir in margarine. Press firmly onto bottom of 9-inch springform pan.

5. Beat cream cheese with electric mixer at high speed until fluffy. Add eggs and flour; beat at high speed until smooth, scraping down side of bowl once. Gradually beat in cream of coconut. Stir in ³/₄ cup toasted coconut with wooden spoon.

6. Pour over crust. Bake 1 hour and 10 minutes or until cheesecake springs back when lightly touched (center will be soft). Carefully loosen cheesecake from edge of pan with spatula. Cool on wire rack; refrigerate until firm. Remove side of pan.

7. Prepare Sweetened Whipped Cream. Spoon into pastry bag fitted with star decorating tip. Pipe around edge of cheesecake. Sprinkle remaining toasted coconut inside whipped cream border.   *Makes 10 to 12 servings*

Step 3. Processing cookies until finely crushed.

Step 5. Adding eggs.

Step 6. Loosening cheesecake from edge of pan.

Maple Sweetheart

1 package (3 ounces) ladyfingers,
    split
2 tablespoons unflavored gelatin
¼ cup cold water
½ cup real maple syrup
5 eggs*
2 cups whipping cream
    Dark brown sugar for garnish

*Use clean, uncracked eggs.

1. Line side of 9-inch springform pan with ladyfingers.

2. Dissolve gelatin in cold water. (Technique on page 23.)

3. Bring maple syrup to a boil over medium heat in small heavy saucepan. Attach candy thermometer to side of pan, making sure bulb is completely submerged in syrup but not touching bottom of pan. Continue boiling until it reaches 230°F. Pour into 1-cup glass measure.

4. Beat eggs in large bowl with electric mixer at high speed until light and fluffy. Gradually add hot syrup mixture in thin stream, beating at high speed until mixture starts to cool and stiff peaks form.

5. Stir in gelatin mixture. Refrigerate about 30 minutes or until mixture mounds slightly when dropped from spoon. (Technique on page 57.)

6. Beat whipping cream until soft peaks form. (Technique on page 56.)

7. Fold 3 cups whipped cream into gelatin mixture with rubber spatula by gently cutting down to bottom of bowl, scraping up side of bowl, then folding over top of mixture. Repeat until whipped cream is evenly incorporated into gelatin mixture.

8. Pour into ladyfinger-lined pan. Refrigerate 2 hours until firm. To serve, remove side of pan. Top dessert with remaining whipped cream. Garnish, if desired. *Makes 10 servings*

Step 1. Lining pan with ladyfingers.

Step 3. Bringing syrup to a boil.

Step 4. Adding hot syrup to beaten eggs.

Angel Cream Dessert

1 package (3 ounces) cream cheese
20 saltine crackers
1½ cups sugar, divided
1 teaspoon baking powder
3 egg whites (technique on page 17)
⅛ teaspoon salt
1½ teaspoons vanilla, divided
½ cup chopped pecans
1 cup miniature marshmallows
¼ cup whipping cream, whipped (technique on page 16)
½ cup sour cream
¼ cup chopped maraschino cherries
Assorted fresh fruit for serving

1. Preheat oven to 350°F. Grease 8-inch round baking pan.

2. Place cream cheese on opened package on cutting board. With utility knife, cut cream cheese lengthwise into ½-inch slices. Then cut crosswise into ½-inch pieces. Let stand at room temperature until softened.

3. Crumble saltines by hand into coarse crumbs. Measure 1 cup; set aside.

4. Combine 1 cup sugar and baking powder; set aside. Beat egg whites and salt in clean large bowl with electric mixer at high speed until foamy. Gradually beat in sugar mixture and vanilla until stiff peaks form. After beaters are lifted from meringue, stiff peaks should remain on surface, and mixture will not slide around when bowl is tilted.

5. Fold in cracker crumbs and pecans with rubber spatula by gently cutting down to bottom of bowl, scraping up side of bowl, then folding over top of mixture. Repeat until crackers are evenly incorporated into meringue. Pour into prepared pan.

6. Bake 30 minutes. Turn off oven and let stand in oven 10 minutes. Remove from oven and cool completely; center will fall. Loosen edge and remove from pan.

7. Combine cream cheese with remaining ½ cup sugar and ½ teaspoon vanilla in large bowl. Beat with electric mixer until smooth.

8. Gently fold in marshmallows, whipped cream, sour cream and cherries as described in step 5. Spread over cooled base; refrigerate. Top with fresh fruit, if desired.

Makes 8 servings

Step 3. Crumbling saltines.

Step 4. Testing for stiff peaks.

Step 6. Loosening edge of cake from pan.

Coconut-Orange Soufflé

2 envelopes unflavored gelatin
½ cup water
4 eggs, separated (technique on page 17)*
½ cup sugar, divided
1 can (15 ounces) Coco Lopez® Cream of Coconut
1 cup pineapple juice
¼ cup creme de cacao (optional)
¼ cup frozen orange juice concentrate, thawed
1 tablespoon bottled lemon juice
½ teaspoon grated orange peel (technique on page 35) (optional)
1½ cups whipping cream
  Orange peel for garnish

*Use clean, uncracked eggs.

1. Tape 3-inch wide waxed paper "collar" around rim of 1½-quart soufflé dish. (Technique on page 57.)

2. Sprinkle gelatin over water in small bowl. Let stand without stirring 3 minutes for gelatin to soften.

3. Beat egg yolks and ¼ cup sugar in small saucepan. Cook over low heat, stirring constantly, until thickened. Add gelatin mixture. Heat over low heat, stirring constantly, until gelatin is completely dissolved, about 5 minutes. (Technique on page 23.)

4. Combine gelatin mixture, cream of coconut, pineapple juice, creme de cacao, orange juice concentrate, lemon juice and orange peel in large bowl. Refrigerate mixture, stirring occasionally. Chill until mixture mounds slightly when dropped from spoon, about 45 minutes. Remove from refrigerator.

5. Beat egg whites until foamy. Gradually beat in remaining ¼ cup sugar until stiff peaks form. (Technique on page 18.)

6. Fold egg whites into gelatin mixture. (Technique on page 56.)

7. Beat whipping cream until soft peaks form. Fold 2 cups whipped cream into gelatin mixture. (Technique on page 56.)

8. Pour mixture into prepared dish. Refrigerate 3 hours or until set.

9. Remove collar. Pipe remaining 1 cup whipped cream on top of soufflé. Garnish, if desired.   *Makes 8 to 10 servings*

Step 3. Testing for undissolved gelatin.

Step 9. Piping whipped cream on top of soufflé.

Tropical Bread Pudding

¾ cup raisins
3 cups milk
3 eggs
1 cup sugar
1 cup shredded coconut
⅔ cup coarsely chopped walnuts
3 tablespoons butter, melted
2 tablespoons vanilla
1 teaspoon ground nutmeg
1 jar (8 ounces) maraschino
   cherries, undrained
1 can (11 ounces) mandarin
   orange segments, undrained
1 loaf (16 ounces) cinnamon-
   raisin bread
   Orange Sauce (recipe follows)

1. Preheat oven to 350°F.

2. Lightly spray 13 × 9-inch baking pan with cooking spray.

3. Place raisins in small bowl. Pour boiling water over to cover. Let stand 2 to 3 minutes or until plump. Drain.

4. Combine raisins, milk, eggs, sugar, coconut, walnuts, butter, vanilla and nutmeg in large bowl; mix well. Add cherries and oranges with liquid; mix well.

5. Break bread into large pieces, about 2 inches square. Add bread pieces to milk mixture. Mixture should be moist but not soupy. Pour into prepared pan. Sprinkle with additional coconut, if desired.

6. Bake 1 hour to 1 hour and 15 minutes or until knife inserted near center comes out clean. Serve with Orange Sauce.

Makes 10 to 12 servings

Orange Sauce

1½ cups powdered sugar
½ cup butter, melted
¼ cup whipping cream
1 egg yolk (technique on page 17)
2 tablespoons orange-flavored liqueur

1. Combine powdered sugar, butter and whipping cream in medium saucepan. Add egg yolk; mix well with wire whisk. Cook over medium heat, stirring constantly, until thickened.

2. Remove from heat and add liqueur. Let cool slightly.

Step 3. Pouring boiling water over raisins.

Step 5. Adding bread pieces to milk mixture.

Step 6. Testing for doneness.

INDEX